P is for Possum

Love Letters from a Forest

by Martha Kelly

Author's Note:
Technically the word is "opossum," but "possum" is the familiar term in these parts. Look up fiddle tunes such as "Possum On a Rail" for more local color.

In loving memory of my mom
Neta Kelly

and for my dad
Ernest Kelly

who together taught me wildflowers,
who tried to teach me birds,
and who introduced me to my first beloved forest.

With grateful thanks to Jude Dippold for editing,
techical assistance, and emotional support.

The illustrations were created in ink and watercolor.

ISBN: 978-1-7357895-7-6
Library of Congress Control Number: 2020921163

Memphis, Tennessee.
www.marthakellyart.com

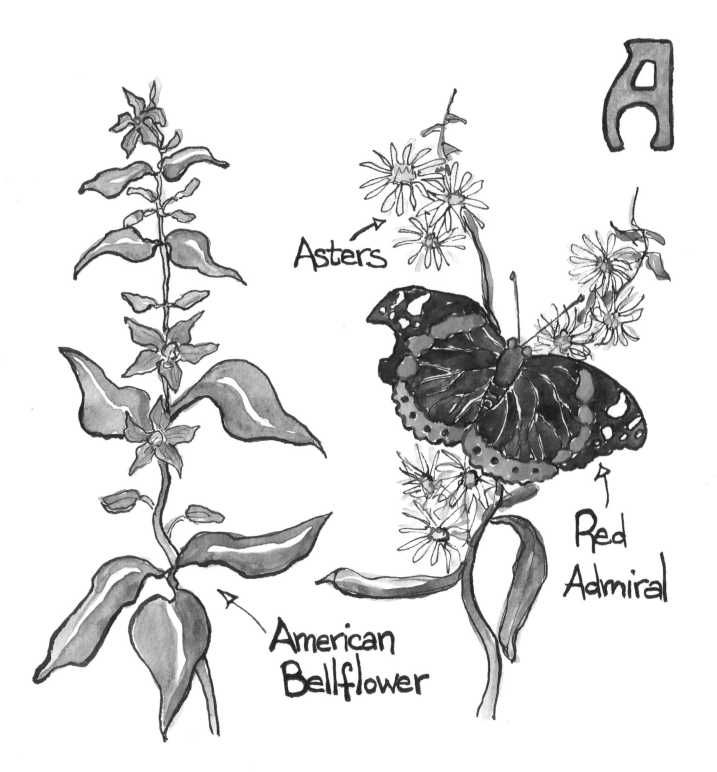

Asters

American
Bellflower

Red
Admiral

A

B

the Barred Owl says "Who cooks for you?"

Cardinals

male

female

C

Celandine
Poppy

Copperhead – watch your step!

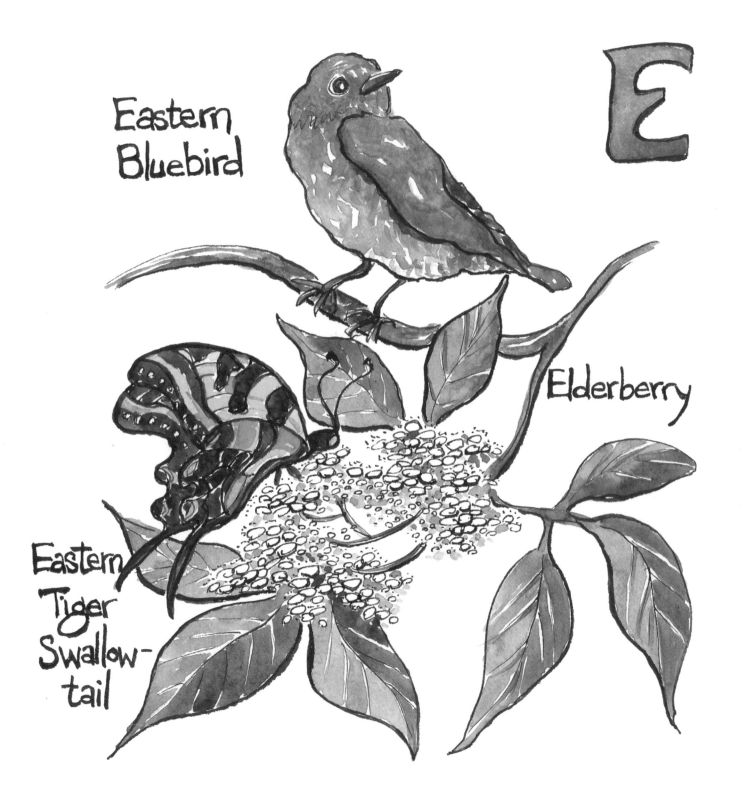

Eastern
Bluebird

E

Elderberry

Eastern
Tiger
Swallow-
tail

F

Fireflies
light up
the evening

Fungi   Fox

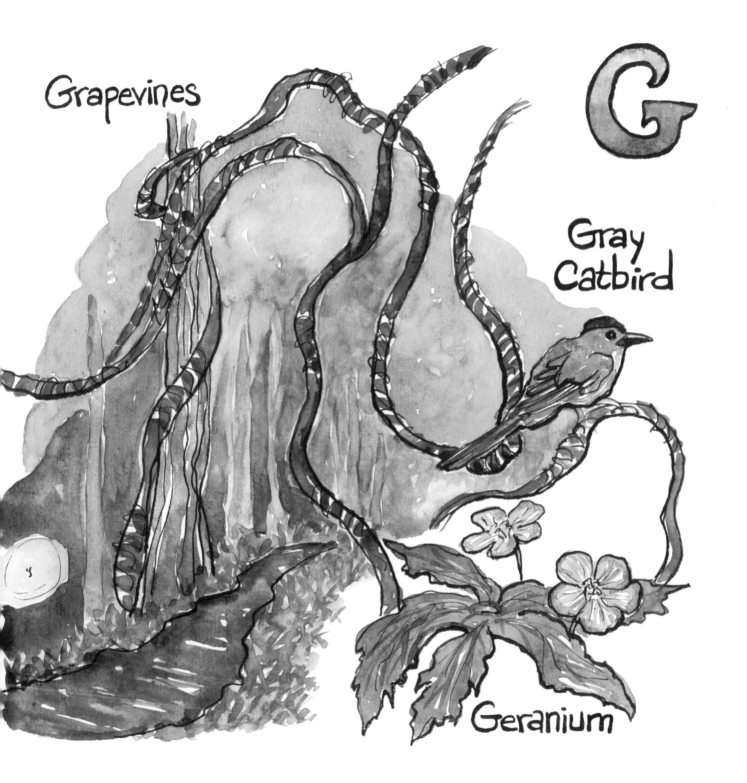

Grapevines

Gray
Catbird

G

Geranium

H

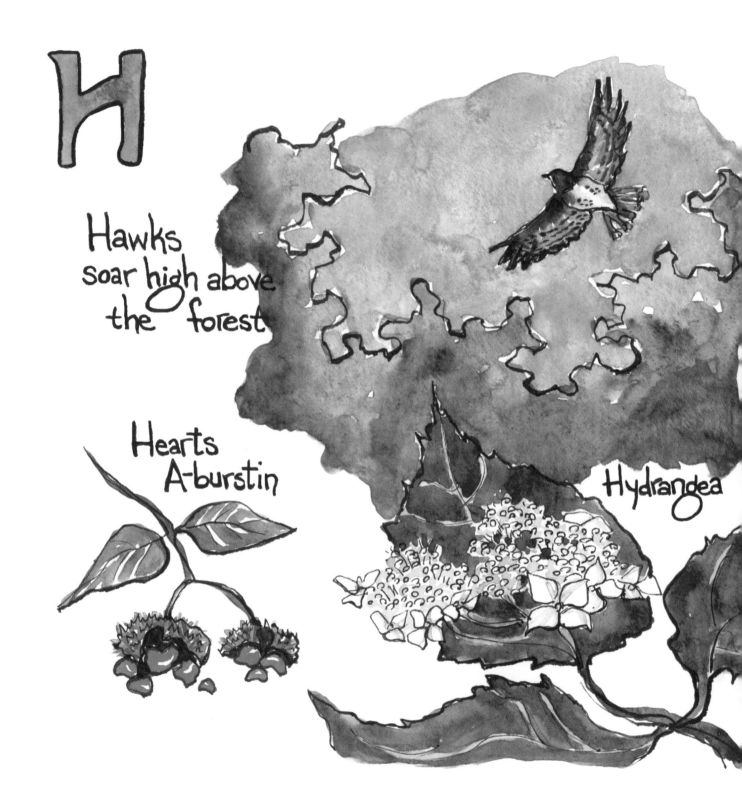

Hawks
soar high above
the forest

Hearts
A-burstin

Hydrangea

Indigo Bunting

Inland Sea Oats

J

Jack in the Pulpit– subtle, striped blooms under three big leaves

Jacob's Ladder

K

Kite

(Mississippi Kite)

Katydid

L

Luna
Moth

Mayapples

blossom
(March to April)

M

Mourning dove —
makes sweet clucking
noises as she flies

apple
(May to June)

N

Northern Parula
tiny warbler
here all summer

Whitebreasted
Nuthatch

here all
year

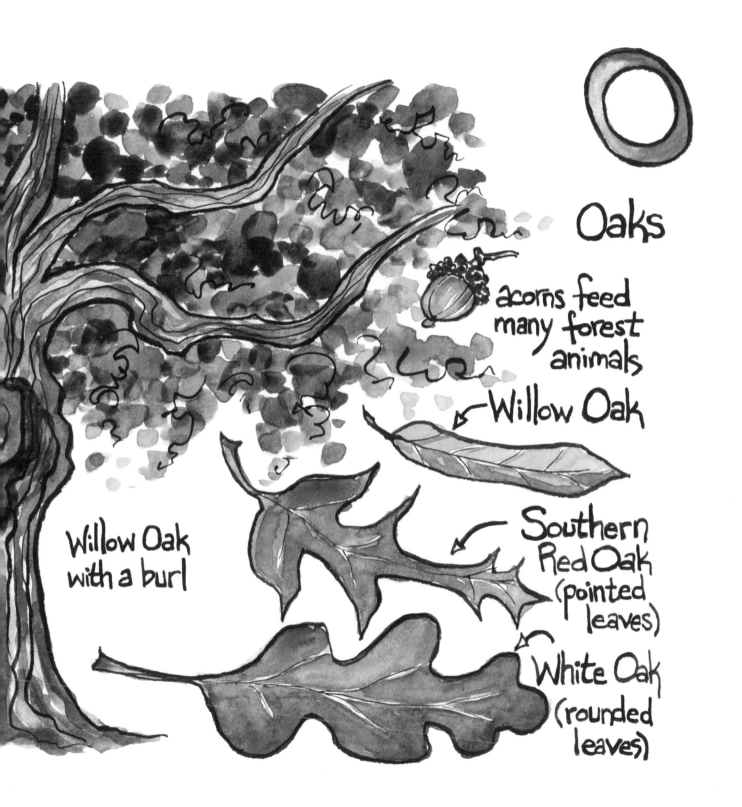

Oaks

acorns feed
many forest
animals

Willow Oak

Willow Oak
with a burl

Southern
Red Oak
(pointed
leaves)

White Oak
(rounded
leaves)

P

Pawpaws—
smallish
trees with
dense, creamy
fruit that
perfumes
the forest

q

Question
Mark butterfly

Possum—
opposable
thumbs
on back
feet for
climbing

Poison Ivy
watch out for hairy
vines and three leaves

R

Rabbits
dart across the
path sometimes

Resurrection Fern
revives from brown to green
with every rain

S

Sycamore

The bark peels off in patches

Sometimes there are hearts

huge, crinkly leaves

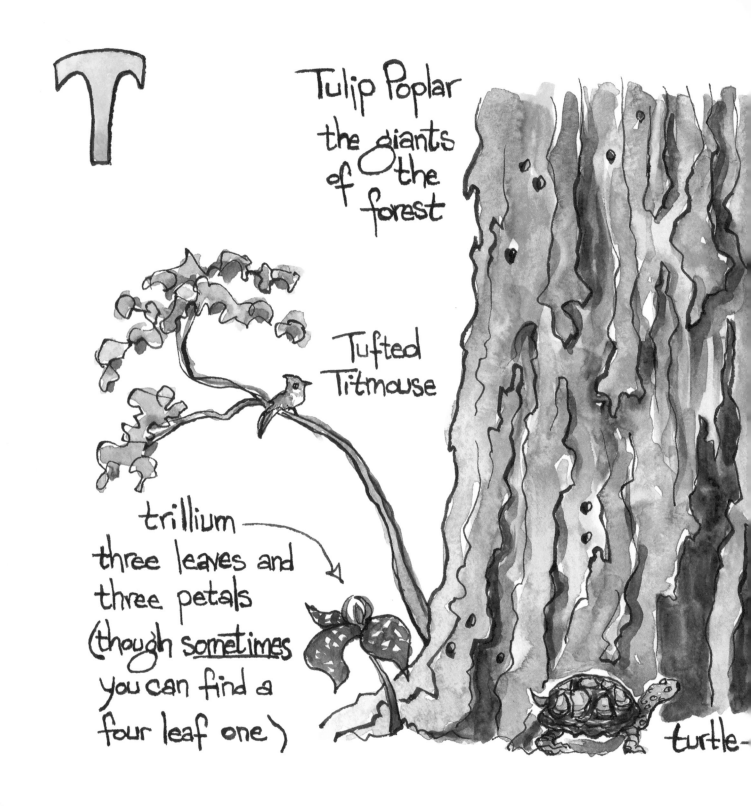

T

Tulip Poplar
the giants
of the
forest

Tufted
Titmouse

trillium
three leaves and
three petals
(though sometimes
you can find a
four leaf one)

turtle

U

Understory —
everything that
grows between the
canopy and the
forest floor

sometimes they'll stop to pose

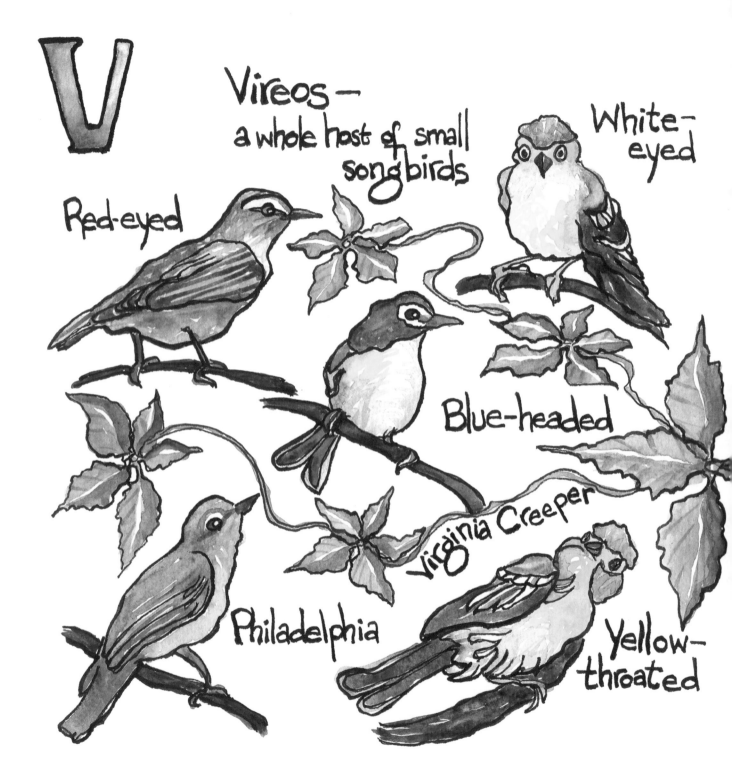

V

Vireos —
a whole host of small
songbirds

White-eyed

Red-eyed

Blue-headed

Virginia Creeper

Philadelphia

Yellow-throated

Downy

Pileated

Wood-
peckers

W

⊲ Red-
bellied

Woodland
Phlox

Y

Yellow
Warbler

Yellow
Sorrel

Z

Zabulon Skipper

Zebra Swallowtail

Martha Kelly lives in her grandparents' house in Midtown Memphis with her companion and four-legged muse Mr. Darcy. They take daily walks in the Old Forest and often stop to sketch. Martha illustrated The Book of Common Worship for the Presbyterian Church (U.S.A.) in 2018. Her first solo museum show was at Dixon Gallery and Gardens in 2015 and she is looking forward to an exhibition at Walter Anderson Museum of Art (WAMA) in 2022. Follow her sketching, printmaking, and painting (or order more copies of this book!) at www.marthakellyart.com.

Here are several quick dog-walk sketches done on site in the forest. The illustrations in this book were based on drawings like these.

Overton Park in Memphis, Tennessee

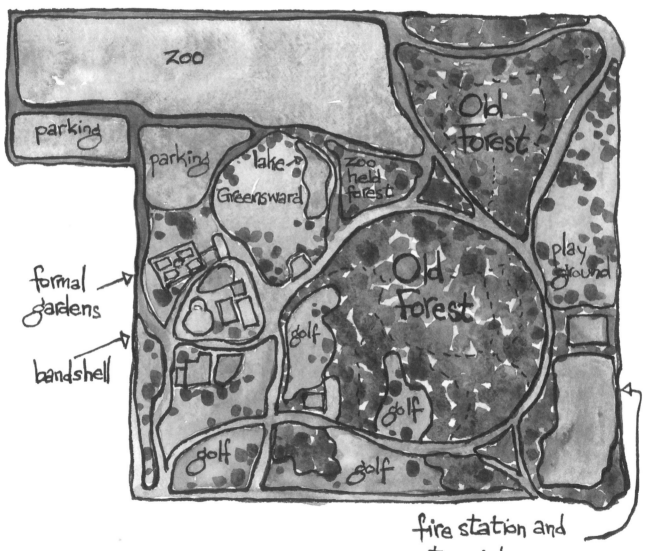

Zoo

parking

parking

lake
Greensward

zoo
held
forest

Old
Forest

formal
gardens

bandshell

golf

Old
Forest

play
ground

golf

golf

golf

fire station and
city maintenance

Overton Park is Memphis's version of Central Park, designed in 1901 by George Kessler to be a refuge from the hardscape of the city. It was originally intended as pure green space, forest and meadows, but the city quickly began developing it with a zoo, art museum, fire station, maintenance facility, and other asphalt added over time. 143 acres of forest remain, only 126 of which are protected. Seventeen acres are in the zoo expansion zone.

My grandmother rode horses on the bridle trails through the forest that Mr. Darcy and I now walk. Hopefully we can keep the current park land and forest green for future generations.

Printed in the USA
CPSIA information can be obtained
at www.ICGtesting.com
LVHW060846181123
764211LV00073B/50